GIRL'S GUIDE TO LOVING YOURSELF

How To Boost Self-Esteem, Increase Self-Love, Let Go of Self-Doubt, and Embrace Who You Are

Jenn Higgins

D1153617

ISBN: 978-1-957590-30-1

For questions, email: Support@AwesomeReads.org

Please consider writing a review!

Just visit: AwesomeReads.org/review

FREE BONUS

SCAN TO GET OUR NEXT BOOK FOR FREE!

TABLE OF CONTENTS

INTRODUCTION

For far too long, and for many reasons, women have struggled to love themselves. Unfortunately, this lack of self-love often begins in childhood, when girls start receiving messages that they aren't good enough or aren't exactly what society tells them they should be. The good news is that you don't have to fall into this trap. You can learn to love yourself; and in fact, learning to love yourself early in your life is vital to your future happiness.

WHAT IS SELF LOVE?

Before you can begin to love yourself, you have to know what self-love is and what it looks like. Self-love is appreciating yourself for who you are and understanding that you aren't supposed to be anyone but yourself, even if others tell you differently.

Self-love will look different for everyone because it's all about what you need individually to take care of yourself. For you, it might mean putting yourself first, being nice to yourself, or talking to and about yourself with love. For others, it might mean setting healthy boundaries, forgiving themselves when they make a mistake, or learning to be true to themselves about what they want in life.

The term "self-love" is often synonymous with "self-care" and requires us to get back to the basics of what we need, both physically and emotionally, to be able to accept ourselves as we are right that minute. We need to listen to our bodies, which might be telling us to get more sleep or to take a break from exercise. We might need to cut back our working or studying hours and do something fun. Or we might need to indulge in a sweet treat we've been denying ourselves.

Self-care is the practice of doing things that are healthy for your own well-being. This practice is as unique as you are and while it might include other people, it doesn't have to. Sometimes, learning to practice self-care is the best way to start loving yourself. After all, if you love yourself, you're going to enjoy spending time with yourself. You might even become your own best friend!

Women in particular strive for perfection, but it's often a skewed view of perfection, one that's unattainable. Not exercising for a day, putting your studying on the back burner for a couple of hours, eating a couple of cookies: We're told these things are not allowed if we want to be perfect. But that's someone else's idea of perfection, and if we're trying to live up to other people's ideals, we will spend our lifetime chasing someone else's happiness instead of our own.

WHY SELF LOVE CAN
BE HARD TO ACHIEVE

All people, men and women, are constantly inundated with messages that they aren't good enough unless they fit into narrow definitions of beauty and personality. But women and girls receive these messages more often, and society's beauty and personality standards are much higher for them than they are for men.

Levels of self-love among girls have always been lower than they should be, but with the proliferation of social media, they have plummeted to all-time lows. Daily, girls receive the message they aren't good enough through the filtered and photoshopped photos they see online and in popular fashion magazines and e-zines.

In these publications and elsewhere, girls are told that a body type that only 5% of women worldwide actually possess is the standard to which they should aspire. They get the message that if they starve themselves to get that thin, undergo serious surgery to get breast implants, and wear revealing clothing, society will reward them with money, love, and fame.

Also, according to these impossibly high standards, girls should be happy and funny and witty at all times. If they aren't, they are considered unlikeable, mean, or bossy and not at all feminine. Of course, that's not the case and women can and do have as many moods as men; they're just expected not to show those moods.

Part of this expectation comes from the traditional view that women are supposed to care for others, so if they're not always happy and smiling, they're not making others happy either. Of course, women don't just exist to please others, but despite all the progress women have made toward being treated as individuals rather than extensions of men, this belief is still pervasive in society.

The truth is that girls should never have to sacrifice their own well-being and happiness to please others in any capacity. Certainly, with the near-constant barrage of messages telling them otherwise, this is much easier said than done. And it's not just the images they see and the almost worshipful attitude society has for celebrities that can derail self-love. All it takes is one snide comment from a group of gossipy "friends" to cause girls to begin questioning themselves and the way they look or think.

Fortunately, there is an antidote to the poison that is society's unreasonable expectations for women's appearance and personality, and it isn't avoiding all media that perpetuates these standards (although limiting exposure to social media and other entertainment publications will help). The solution is to teach girls like you from an early age how to love themselves and not settle for less than they deserve.

BENEFITS OF
SELF LOVE

When you love someone, you treat that person with compassion and care. You give them gifts that make them feel loved and you speak to them kindly (most of the time). You want them to be happy so you'll do what you can to make that happen.

Loving yourself is no different.

We are so much more critical of ourselves than we are of anybody else that we may end up thinking we're not worthy of love. But that couldn't be further from the truth. We deserve to treat ourselves like any other person we love and care for. When we practice self-love, we gain a multitude of benefits that we can't get any other way.

Greater Happiness

Loving yourself leads to a higher sense of well-being, which in turn, makes you feel happier. You no longer have to compare yourself to others or strive for something you don't really want because you're being true to your own desires and feelings. You aren't trying and failing to live up to some impossible standard that wasn't even yours to begin with.

Your relationships with others will be better because when you treat yourself the way you expect others to treat you, there won't be any room for disrespect, mistreatment, or toxicity. If someone doesn't respect your boundaries, you will love yourself enough to release that person from your life, thereby making your life happier.

Much of our anxiety and stress come from the fear of failure and not living up to others' expectations. Loving yourself means living up to your own expectations, which are really the only ones you can control anyway. Knowing that your self-worth is not dependent upon others' opinions and expectations removes the elements of anxiety and stress from your shoulders. Without anxiety and stress, your body feels and performs better. And if your body feels good, you feel good.

Stronger Resilience

Everyone experiences challenges throughout life, and how we respond to those challenges is a reflection of self-love. Experts have shown that the more people loves themselves, the more capable they are of coming out stronger on the other side of a hardship, and those who love themselves generally rebound more quickly as well.

This could be because people who know their self-worth don't allow themselves to obsess over their failures or turn to dangerous coping mechanisms like alcohol, drugs, or other risky behaviors to get them through the tough times. They know they aren't defined by their failure, but instead by what they learn from it. They take the opportunity to grow and learn instead of using their failure as an excuse to quit.

This doesn't mean that if you love yourself, you won't ever be sad, disappointed, scared, or angry. It just means that you'll allow yourself to feel those emotions, acknowledge them as a part of who you are, and move past them when they no longer serve a purpose, when they're keeping you back from personal growth.

And, when you make a mistake in your life, you'll be quicker to forgive yourself, just as you would another person you love. You'll also have a more positive mindset that things will work out for the best, which isn't always the case when you don't love yourself. Without that self-love, it's too easy to fall into the trap of thinking you're a bad person because you made a mistake instead of understanding that you're human and are going to make mistakes.

Improved Mental and Physical Health

As previously mentioned, when you no longer have a crushing amount of anxiety and stress, you feel better. Some stress is actually good for you, as it keeps you alert and helps you avoid danger, but too much stress leads to physical and mental pain. According to physicians, stress can cause headaches, upset stomach, high blood pressure, insomnia, and even chest pain.

Likewise, untreated anxiety can lead to panic attacks, headaches, a pounding heart, breathing problems, depression, upset stomach, muscle aches, and high blood pressure. In essence, stress and anxiety about fitting in, meeting unreasonable expectations, and making mistakes can cause your body to respond through pain because it is telling you something is wrong. Your body wants you to figure out the cause of this pain and relieve it.

This doesn't mean that if you love yourself then you won't have any stress or anxiety. After all, you will always be a little anxious before you try something new or when you're facing an important decision, but the stress and anxiety levels will be normal instead of out of whack. Your body will respond to them appropriately, allowing you to deal with the intense situation appropriately, with focus and motivation.

Additionally, when you love yourself, you want to treat yourself right. This means you'll be more apt to get an appropriate amount of sleep each night, to eat healthy, and to exercise. Loving yourself means loving the body you have and giving it what it needs to function at its best. Sleeping well, eating well, and exercising often will all make you healthier over time.

And being healthy is not the same for everyone. Certainly, there are medical guidelines for what is considered healthy, but those guidelines are just that: guidelines. They aren't hard and fast rules and they aren't meant to tell everyone they should look or weigh the same. They are designed to help your body function optimally according to scientific standards. But no matter what you read or see or hear, discuss your health with a doctor so you can understand what's best for you and take the appropriate steps to achieve your personal standard of health.

Increased Motivation

Speaking of motivation, learning to love yourself will increase your motivation to reach your goals. Self-love breeds confidence, which you need to be able to take the steps toward achieving what you want in life. You'll be less afraid of failing because you'll know that failure is just a part of success and it doesn't mean you should stop trying. In fact, the more you fail, the more you'll appreciate your eventual success.

Viewing a setback as a temporary situation allows you to move forward instead of getting stuck in obsessing over your failures. And self-love gives you the desire to overcome those setbacks and the confidence to know you can. Building confidence in girls has long been challenging, mostly because many people think it's something others have to give to them. But it's not. Confidence is something that can only come from self-love: learning to trust, forgive, and believe in yourself.

Motivation is a part of resilience in that the more motivated you are to do something, the quicker you can move past the difficult times in your life. But motivation is also about the ability to change your circumstances by setting goals and making a plan to achieve them. You can either accept what life gives you and love yourself where you are, or, if you don't like where you are, you can work to change it. Either way, when you love yourself, you're motivated to accept things or you're motivated to change them.

This guide intends to teach girls how to love themselves at an early age so they have the skills to combat any negative messages they might receive throughout their lives. By learning self-love when you are young, you'll be able to quickly identify sabotaging behaviors and apply techniques to prevent them from harming your confidence or slipping into negative thought patterns. This guide will introduce these sabotaging behaviors, discuss where and why those behaviors occur, explain why they shouldn't occur, and provide self-love tips for halting them.

CHAPTER ONE:
THE DANGERS
OF COMPARISON

A major barrier to self-love is something nearly everyone does at least some of the time. We compare ourselves to others or a curated image of others, and unfortunately, we usually find ourselves lacking. We think we aren't as good as the people we see in our lives, whether that's because we don't have as much money as they do or our family looks different than theirs does, or we are dealing with issues that no one else appears to be dealing with.

It's natural to look at other people in your life and compare your qualities and accomplishments to theirs. But what happens is we end up comparing our *average* qualities and accomplishments to their *best* qualities and accomplishments. This means we'll never measure up and that's damaging to our view of ourselves.

After all, is it fair to make someone who is left-handed write a letter with their right hand? No, and that's why we shouldn't compare unlike qualities and accomplishments (even if they seem alike) with others. It's self-destructive and unproductive.

WHERE WE DO IT

Humans compare themselves with others in all facets of life, but it's most noticeable in areas of life where we find our peers. For example, if you're a student, you're naturally going to compare yourself with other students around your age. If you're an athlete, you're likely going to compare yourself with other people who are athletes, and specifically, the athletes that participate in the same activities.

This means that comparisons are made wherever our peers are: at school, in the gym, online, at neighborhood functions, on television, at work, and more. The impulse to make these comparisons is natural and strong, so you will really have to fight against the urge to do it, especially since we've long been raised to look at others and determine how we stack up. Not only that, but many constructs are in place to facilitate those comparisons.

For example, teachers are required to grade students to understand how well students are comprehending their lessons. Unfortunately, this sets up a means of comparison for students, who naturally want to know what grade everyone else earned so they can see where they fall. Likewise, standardized test scores are all about comparing how well or poorly students of the same age and grade are performing.

In sports, we compare ourselves to elite athletes, particularly those who are at or around our own age. It doesn't matter if we logically understand that everyone has different athletic abilities or that we might be better at one skill than they are. We compare our deficits to their strengths even though there's no way that's an equal comparison and we're going to fall short no matter what.

Online comparisons are even worse, but a lot more pervasive. We see other people living lives we think are perfect. After all, we only see what the other people want us to see. Sure, some people air all their dirty laundry online, but most people don't and as such, we think we're comparing a perfect life with our own not-so-perfect life. Again, logically, we know that no one has a perfect life, but our inner voice becomes critical anyway, saying we don't measure up.

In the gym, we see people whose physiques are more in line with society's beauty standard and we wonder why we can't achieve that, even if we're working out and eating right. We see some people who seem to eat whatever they want and never gain an ounce of weight and it doesn't seem fair. What we don't see is how hard they may have worked to get where they are or we don't understand that everyone's body is different, and none is better or worse than the other.

Television programs and entertainment publications are full of stories about remarkable people who have accomplished much more (or so it seems) than we have. We question our commitment to our goals and wonder why it's so easy for other people but so hard for us. What we don't see, though, is that perhaps those people had certain advantages we don't have or they were lucky enough to have a break that we just haven't had yet.

Comparisons are everywhere and we subconsciously make them whether we realize it or not. Our brain processes information so quickly that we can make a negative comparison in a split second and before we know it, we're already telling ourselves we're not good enough.

WHY WE DO IT

Comparisons are not inherently bad. They can be a catalyst for growth and self-improvement and, sometimes, comparing yourself to others can be useful for identifying things you still need to learn. But you have to be careful that you're comparing apples to apples. What does this mean? It means that you have to make sure you're comparing like things about you and the other person so you can identify places you can improve. In other words, if all things are equal (education levels, ages, experience, etc.), you can compare a specific quality or achievement to another person's.

But, if even one thing is unequal, the comparison may not be fair. And this is where these comparisons can be detrimental. For instance, you might think that your grade on a math test is comparable to your friend's grade on that same math test because you're both the same age and the test is covering the same material.

However, unless you both got the same amount of sleep the night before the test, you both had a good breakfast, you both mastered the same exact math skills required to take the test, and you both took the test in the exact same environments, the comparisons are unequal. As such, most comparisons are invalid because there are too many variables involved.

We're Socialized to Be Competitive

Yet, humans are designed to make these comparisons. We are socialized to be competitive, to do better than others in every area possible. We want to achieve what others have, especially if we think their lives are better. When we "win" a comparison, our brain releases feel-good hormones that make us happy. As such, we continue chasing that feeling by comparing ourselves to almost everyone we meet.

But our lives are not games. There doesn't have to be a winner and a loser, even though we are socialized to think there should be. Everyone can win at self-love if we know how to stop comparing ourselves to others. If our society valued helping everyone realize their best self instead of valuing only winners, there would be no need for a guide like this. Fortunately, you can opt out of the competition and start finding other ways to get your brain to release those feel-good hormones.

We're Naturally Envious

We are also naturally envious, so if we see another person doing something we want to do, or buying something we want to have, we strive to meet or exceed that person's achievements. This isn't necessarily bad because it can motivate us to do better and make changes in our lives to get what we want, but over the long term, always coveting another person's achievements will eventually become a demotivator.

Someone is always going to have more than you do or be able to do more. Endless envy leads to self-hatred because envy is defined by viewing yourself in terms of what you don't have. There will always be something you want and don't have, and if you define your self-worth on this basis, you'll never be fulfilled.

We Want to Fit In

One reason why adolescent girls compare themselves to others is the desire to fit in. They see the fashions that the "popular" girls wear and the activities they participate in. They make the connection that these "things" and activities are what make these girls popular, even if that's not the truth. These comparisons can often pressure you to do things you might ordinarily not do and can actually be dangerous.

For instance, if another girl in your class is drinking alcohol at a party and you associate her with popularity, you might be more likely to drink alcohol as well. What you're doing is comparing yourself with her and determining what you aren't doing that you think you should be doing to be as popular as she is. Not only are you telling yourself that without alcohol you're not as good as she is, but you're also making a choice to engage in a dangerous activity in an attempt to be her equal in other people's eyes.

While comparing ourselves to others is natural, it's not good for our mental health, especially if the comparisons are demotivating instead of motivating. Even then, you're still subconsciously telling yourself that you're not as good as someone else, if only for a while.

Instead, the best comparison to make, and the only one that really matters, is to yourself. Compare your current self to your past self to see if you've become more like the person you want to become, if you've achieved your goals, if you've mastered a skill. When you focus on becoming the person you want to be instead of trying to be like someone else, you're practicing self-love.

WHY WE SHOULDN'T DO IT

We Can't Be Anyone but Ourselves

The most obvious reason why we shouldn't compare ourselves to others is that we simply can't be anyone but ourselves. Every single person is unique, which means every comparison you make between you and another person is not entirely fair. We all have special skills and strengths, and what comes easy to one person may be difficult to another.

This doesn't mean we shouldn't work on ourselves to become better people, but it does mean that what a "better person" looks like is not found in other people. It's found inside each person and is different for each person. Your better person might be kinder and more empathetic while another person's "better person" has a fulfilling job that allows them to pursue their passion. Neither "better person" is right or wrong. It's just about what values you have and what makes you feel good about yourself.

We Find Ourselves Lacking

We're also bound to find ourselves lacking if we compare ourselves to too many people, especially if we're not comparing like things (apples to apples). When we compare our weaknesses to other people's strengths, we're only going to feel worse about ourselves.

Sure, this might be motivating to some degree, making us work harder to become better at a specific skill. But if we never get to that other person's level or we do achieve it only to begin comparing another weakness to someone else's strength, we're going to dislike that part of ourselves even more.

We Don't See the Whole Picture

What we must keep in mind is that comparisons with other people are usually invalid. We don't see the entire picture of what we're comparing. For instance, if you compare the vacation your friend took to Hawaii this summer with your trip to Kansas, you might think you're comparing like items and that your trip was much less exciting than your friend's. On the surface, that might be true, but what if you knew that this was the first trip your friend has ever taken, while you have traveled to different states every summer you can remember?

Certainly, the trip to Hawaii sounds like a great time, but would you rather travel once in your life to one spectacular place or many times to various locations, having different experiences every summer? When you understand the full picture, you might see that your trip to Kansas isn't at all comparable to your friend's trip to Hawaii.

We Focus on the Wrong Things

Humans are also conditioned to obsess over the things we don't have instead of appreciating the things we do have. We always want more or better: more money, belongings, achievements, clothes, cars, jobs, and it's difficult for us to be happy with what we already have.

When we only see what we're lacking instead of what we have, we're always going to feel inferior. And our society is very materialistic and promotes the idea that one must accumulate things to show how successful they are. But the saying "you can't take it with you" is appropriate here. When you die, do you want to be known as a person who had all the things or a person who loved themselves and others? A shift in mindset to appreciation instead of want can help us love ourselves for what we already have and are.

HOW TO STOP
DOING IT

It's very difficult to stop doing something we've been conditioned and socialized to do, and comparing ourselves to others is no different. We have to completely change the way we think about other people and their lives. Instead of competing with others, we need to compete only with ourselves, striving to become the people we want to be instead of trying to be someone else.

Avoid Triggers

To begin with, we need to identify our triggers and learn how to avoid them. If we're always comparing our body to other people's bodies, for instance, and it's making us feel bad about the way we look, we need to avoid situations that set us up for those comparisons. Maybe we stop reading entertainment and fashion publications or perhaps we join a body-positive community that celebrates all types of bodies instead of a single idealized figure.

If we find ourselves feeling bad about not having the type or quality of belongings that other people have, maybe we need to limit what we see in our social media feeds to people who don't make us feel that way. You won't be able to avoid all your triggers, especially in places like school, but if there are some people who tend to brag about their belongings or put you down because of yours, it's definitely possible for you to avoid those people specifically. If you can't do it on your own, ask your parents and teachers for help.

Limit Social Media

Social media is one of the biggest offenders when it comes to feeding into unfair comparisons. The best thing to do to combat these false comparisons is to limit the time you spend online looking at others' profiles, posts, and comments. Remember that you're only seeing what your friends want you to see (the same is true in person, but it's harder to hide imperfections in person than it is from behind a computer).

If you think about an iceberg, the tip that's sticking out of the water is the amount of information you have from an online post or profile. The entire part of the iceberg that's underwater is everything you're not seeing, and without that other information, you can't possibly make an apples-to-apples comparison. Let's look at an example.

You see a post from a friend who's been gifted a new car for their 16th birthday. You compare your life to theirs because you don't have a new car, or any car for that matter. You start thinking that your life is not as good as your friend's because you don't have a car and that maybe you're not as worthy as your friend of getting a car because otherwise why would they just be gifted one without having to work for it?

The key to halting these negative thought patterns is to think of the iceberg theory. What you see is that your friend got a car for their birthday. What you don't see is everything else in your friend's life that could have gone into getting that car. Below the surface, the iceberg plunges deep, and maybe what you don't see is:

- Your friend's parents recently split up and the car was a gift to make a parent feel less guilty about that
- Your friend's parents took out a loan to get the car instead of saving that money for your friend's future college expenses
- Your friend's parents have been saving for years to have the money to buy this expensive gift for their child
- Your friend's family places a higher value on a nice car than other expenses in their lives (perhaps they rent their home instead of owning it or they have fewer other belongings because they love cars)

If you have these other pieces of information, you are better equipped to make an equal comparison. You can see that even though your friend has a brand new car, maybe there are other things going on in the friend's life that aren't as good. Or maybe their family has different values than your family has.

The point is that your friend probably won't post everything about their life just so you can make a fair comparison. Instead, you just shouldn't make a comparison at all because you don't see the entire picture. This is easier said than done, though, so the next best thing is to limit your exposure to these posts or stay off social media altogether.

Everyone Struggles

A related tip to helping you avoid making comparisons with other people is to remember that everyone has struggles, even if you don't see them. That iceberg image can be used for so many parts of life, from what it takes to succeed to what we see on social media, to what a person is feeling at any given time.

We all tend to put on a good face for other people because we care what they think (more on this later), but no life is perfect and that submerged part of the iceberg is often more revealing than the tip. This is also why most people prefer to keep the biggest part of the iceberg underwater. They fear that if they show others everything they're hiding, they won't be liked or accepted anymore.

Moreover, it's long been taboo in many cultures to discuss struggles with other people. Privacy, especially in the U.S., is highly valued and sharing too much about our personal lives is considered attention-seeking behavior. So, instead, we put on a happy face and share only the good things about our lives. What this does, though, is make other people think their lives are not nearly as good because they believe they're the only one going through challenging things.

List What You're Grateful For

An excellent way to get past the feeling that other people always have more than you do is to make a list of things you have and are grateful for. When you can visualize all the things you own or have accomplished in your life, you may realize that you have way more than you thought you did. Your list might not be as long as others' lists, but that doesn't matter. What you're looking at when you do this exercise is how rich your life already is.

You can also spend some time with people who are less fortunate than you are to help you appreciate what you have in your life even more. Volunteering at a homeless shelter, working with underprivileged kids, reading stories about people living in poorer countries, and organizing donations for people who have lost everything in a fire or other natural disaster can really open your eyes to how great your life is and how fortunate you are that your circumstances are better than many other situations.

Reframe Competition as Motivation

One reason why comparisons to other people is so damaging to our mental health is because we look at our lives as a competition. Who can achieve more? Who can make more money? Who can get into the best college? Who can make the highest grade? Only one person can win these competitions and when it's not you, it can make you feel like a failure.

Instead of looking at comparisons as a competition of who is the best person based on arbitrary standards, try viewing comparisons as motivation for you to do better. This doesn't mean you're going to beat the person you're comparing yourself to. It just means that you admire something about them that you want for yourself. You may achieve the same level that the other person has achieved, but if you can incorporate some of what you admire about them in your own life, you're doing something good for yourself.

Identify What You are Proud Of

Keeping in mind that no two people are exactly the same, there are certainly things about you or things that you've done that you should be proud of. Even if they're small accomplishments or what you view as unimportant skills or abilities, you should take pride in your differences. What do you do well that other people struggle with? What is your favorite physical feature? What have you accomplished in school that is helping you progress toward your life goals?

No matter how insignificant you think something is, if you're proud of it, list it. This will help you see that you are an amazing person already and you don't need to try to live up to what others are doing. Of course, you can always improve in certain areas of your life, but never lose sight of what you have already done or who you already are while you're striving for that improvement.

When you start to feel like you haven't accomplished anything or that other people are leaving you behind, this list of what you're proud of will bring you back to the truth: that you're just as incredible as they are in your own ways. Reminding yourself of what you have already accomplished in life is a form of self-love and will only make you appreciate yourself more.

Celebrate Others' Successes

When you don't view everything as a competition, you can genuinely feel happy for other people's successes. And as a bonus, you'll feel happier yourself because emotions are contagious. Negativity breeds negativity, so if you're jealous or resentful of another person's achievements, you'll only perpetuate those negative feelings by focusing on what the other person has done that you haven't.

On the other hand, when you celebrate another person's success, you generate the feel-good hormones that put you in a positive state of mind. Maybe you'll start working toward an achievement of your own so you can keep that feeling alive. Or perhaps you'll recall successes you've had in the past and bask in the recurrence of the great feelings you had at the time.

By celebrating others, you're taking away the energy required to compare yourself to them. You can't authentically celebrate someone's success while resenting it at the same time. Letting go of the need to always measure up to other people and their accomplishments will give you the freedom to just be yourself.

Compare Your Current Self with Your Past Self

As previously mentioned, the only person you should compare yourself to is your past self. If you're making progress toward the person you want to be, then there's no reason to measure yourself against other people. You set your own standards for accomplishments, body image, possessions, and more, and those goals should take priority in everything you do.

If you see something another person has that you want, that's fine as long as you use it for motivation to improve yourself and your life and not as proof of something you lack. Again, reframing these comparisons as motivation instead of competition is the key to keeping the comparisons healthy. And if you ever start to feel like you're not as good as the person you're comparing yourself to, then it's no longer motivating and should be forgotten as quickly as possible.

CHAPTER TWO:

WORRYING ABOUT WHAT OTHER PEOPLE THINK

We are a social species that depends on social interaction to survive and thrive. Often, our happiness is contingent on the quality of our relationships with others and nearly every activity we do in life involves other people. As the recent pandemic and the resulting quarantines proved, humans don't do very well without frequent interaction with others. And when we don't get the socialization we need, we may feel lonely and sad.

Of course, this innate desire to socialize with others means we desperately want to belong with other members of our species. As such, we worry about what others think of us more often than is healthy. Moreover, we observe that people who don't follow social norms aren't always accepted by those who do and we don't want to be ostracized because others think we're weird.

Our fear of ostracization causes us to worry about what others think of us. We don't want to embarrass ourselves in front of others or do something that makes us feel ashamed because those behaviors feed our fear of being cast out of a social group. As a result, we constantly monitor our behavior in relation to other people's opinions.

Unfortunately, this causes us to always worry about whether or not we're living up to other people's expectations. And often, just as when we're comparing ourselves to others, we come up short. We do or say something that isn't "right" and suddenly we're wondering if we're going to be dropped from our social relationships. Maybe we wear the wrong clothing label or we tell a joke that no one laughs at. When we don't get the welcoming reaction we want from our social group, we start worrying about what they're *really* thinking.

WHEN WE DO IT

Most of us worry about what other people think about us in all kinds of situations. This can be at school, work, church, at a party, online, anywhere. We often hide parts of ourselves that we think are "uncool" or "weird" because we think others won't accept us for liking certain activities, clothes, music, or other interests.

At school and online are two of the most common places where girls worry about what others think of them because that's where their social groups usually exist. Teens rarely show their true selves at school or online because they are taking cues from their peers. This is why online platforms spawn trend after trend. People see others doing or wearing things that are getting views and likes and they want to fit in by following along.

Selfies are another way that people show they care about what others think. Very rarely these days do teens post unfiltered photographs or candid shots of themselves. Instead, they make sure the pictures they post are carefully posed and edited to ensure they look the way they think other people want them to look. And if they don't get the attention they hope to get through likes, comments, and shares, they worry about why they aren't getting it.

At school, clothes have always been important for many kids, especially girls. Wearing the "right" labels can mean the difference between acceptance and ostracization. This is why many schools enforce uniforms instead of allowing students to wear whatever they want. There is a theory that when everyone has to wear the same clothes, students can't judge each other by what they wear.

Unfortunately, kids seem to always find reasons to exclude others, so the key to battling against this tendency is to learn not to care so much about what others think of you. It's definitely not easy because we want to be accepted and fit in. This is one of our most basic emotional needs. But when we can be our true selves instead of what others want us to be, we find our tribe, the people who like us for who we are.

WHY WE DO IT

We Want to Be Liked and Accepted

We already touched on why we care what other people think about us in the above paragraphs, but essentially, it all comes down to the fact that we want to be liked and we want to belong. It's human nature to want to be liked and accepted and that desire has its roots in our early fights for survival. When humans had to hunt, gather, find shelter, make fire, and defend themselves every single day, they learned it was easier to do in a group than alone.

Our brains still hold onto the idea that need to be a part of a group to survive, even though many of us could survive alone today if we absolutely had to (as long as we have access to all the conveniences of modern life, of course). We are basically hardwired to seek acceptance and avoid rejection. Internally, we are afraid that if we stray too far from "normal," we will be cast out and forced to make it through life on our own.

We Desire Others' Approval

Additionally, we are socialized to believe that the approval of others is necessary for our self-worth. We need to take a minute here and discuss the difference between self-worth and self-esteem because many people use these two terms interchangeably, even though they have very different meanings.

Self-worth is a deep sense of one's own value as a human being and how much value one adds to the world. It is internal and necessary for self-love. On the other hand, self-esteem is more variable. Self-esteem is your thoughts and beliefs about yourself, and can change based on mood and circumstance. When you're having a bad day, your self-esteem might feel lower than on a good day, but your basic self-worth remains the same.

When we care about others' opinions, we are trying to boost our self-esteem, but when we don't get the praise or acceptance we seek, it can damage our self-worth. We internalize these opinions and let them chip away at our sense of worthiness. And if we pay attention to too many negative opinions, we can lose our self-worth entirely.

Unfortunately, this pattern of seeking others' praise to increase our self-esteem and internalizing rejection that decreases self-worth is the recipe behind bullying. Bullies tend to express negative opinions to people they feel don't measure up in some way to get an instant boost to their own self-esteem (i.e., they feel superior to the person they're putting down). But they don't realize that their words impact the receiving person by slowly destroying their self-worth.

People Think About Us Less Than We Believe

We also care about what others think about us because of our own egos. Our behaviors, actions, and attitudes are important to us, so we think they should be important to everyone. Newsflash: they're not. It might be a blow to your ego to discover that people really don't think about you as often as you fear they do. They are usually more concerned about themselves and what others are thinking about them, just like you are.

For instance, think about the last time you embarrassed yourself in front of others. You may have been preoccupied with thinking about or replaying that incident hours or maybe even days. But the people who witnessed it likely forgot about it within minutes. Or they may have thought about it later if they retold the incident to someone else, but that was probably the extent of it.

This is why embarrassing situations that we're involved in fade for others as they move onto new things to worry about, while we might not get past the embarrassment for quite some time. When we realize that people don't think about us as often or for as long as we think they do, we can also move past worrying about their opinions quite so much.

WHY WE
SHOULDN'T DO IT

We Are Inhibiting Our True Selves

While keeping your self-worth as high as it deserves to be is the main reason you should stop worrying so much about what others think of you, it's not the only reason. For one, when we change our behavior or personality to make sure others like us, we aren't being our true selves. We are trying to be someone we're not just because we seek someone else's approval. And when we're always acting, we aren't loving who we really are.

It's Exhausting

Plus, it's exhausting to try to keep up an act. It takes a huge amount of energy to keep your mask in place at all times. You physically aren't designed to be anyone other than yourself, so pretending to be something you're not can eventually manifest in illness, both physical and emotional. Notice how relaxed you are when you're by yourself or with people who know the real you. That's how you should feel almost all the time.

As we get older, we tend to stop pretending we're something we're not, at least most of the time. We get tired of doing it and we realize we'd rather be friends with people who like us for who we are than with people we have to put on an act for. So, to some degree, maturity plays a role in getting tired of pretending, but the earlier you realize it's not worth the effort, the better off you'll be because you'll learn to love yourself sooner.

People Are Liking Something or Someone You're Not

When you present yourself as someone you're not with other people, you're giving them what you think they want, but what's actually happening is that they're liking someone they don't really know. They don't have an opportunity to discover your amazing true self and that's not good for you or for them. They're missing out on knowing a unique person who has a lot to offer and are instead getting a person who doesn't really exist.

We Can't Make Everyone Happy All the Time

You aren't going to make everyone happy all the time and some people aren't going to like you. It's just a fact of life and there's really nothing we can do about it. Once you get past the desire to please everyone, you can focus on just making yourself happy. You can stop hiding who you are when you're around others, and the great thing about this is that you'll find people who like you for the exact things you've been hiding.

We Might Miss Out on Activities We Enjoy

This world is big enough for everyone and there is a place for you. When you pretend to be someone you aren't, you forego opportunities and experiences that you might really enjoy because you're worried about what others might think.

For example, if you really like dressing up like a pirate and attending your local Renaissance Festival, you could miss out on all the fun at the fair if you're focused on the people who think it's "nerdy" to participate in such an event. Trying to fit yourself into someone else's puzzle is impossible and it will just frustrate you and leave you feeling sad and disappointed.

Instead, keep doing the things that make you happy. After all, you're the one who has to live with yourself all the time. Other people can think whatever they want, but their opinion shouldn't prevent you from living your best life. And that best life looks different for everyone, even those people you're trying to impress.

HOW TO STOP DOING IT

Learning to stop caring about what others think of you is truly the key to happiness. That's why it's so hard to do, but if you can at least lessen your worry, you can start on the path toward self-love. The first step is understanding that our desire to belong and to have people like us is innate. It's something we are programmed to do because, at one time, our survival depended on it. Once you realize that your brain is tricking you into this trap, you can maneuver around it.

Be Kind and Considerate to Others and Yourself

Of course, you're not going to stop worrying about what others think of you overnight. It's something you have to train your brain to do. In the meantime, as you work on shifting your perspective, focus on being kind and considerate at all times. People naturally like others who are nice and thoughtful. We are drawn to people who make us feel good about ourselves, so striving to demonstrate those qualities will make you inherently likable.

Being kind and considerate is something you should want to be as a human anyway and you'll discover that as you express your kindness to others, you'll be more likely to express it toward yourself as well. You deserve your own kindness and consideration just as much as others do, so regularly practicing these qualities externally will translate into increased levels of self-love.

Others' Negative Opinions Reflect Themselves

Remember that when people need to boost their self-esteem, they often do it by trying to make themselves look better than others. They may be low on self-worth or are feeling hurt in some way. They lash out at others by putting them down, which gives their self-esteem a quick lift. Certainly, this isn't the right way to gain self-esteem, but many people don't know how to get it any other way.

You may not be able to stop yourself from feeling bad when someone expresses a negative opinion of you, but recognizing that their comment really isn't about you in the first place can help you move past it more quickly. Of course, if the person who made the comment is someone you consider a friend or a person you admire, it will be more difficult to just brush it off, but the key is to really think about whether someone who puts you down is really your friend after all.

Focus Less on Mistakes and Embarrassment

Mistakes are a part of life, but we often try to hide or diminish them because we believe we won't be accepted if others know we aren't perfect. And even though we logically know that no one is perfect, many people still strive for that ideal. This need to be perfect means that any failure we experience is internalized as a flaw that lessens our worthiness.

Try to start viewing your mistakes as opportunities to progress toward the person you want to be. Keep in mind that most people will forgive mistakes as long as you own them and accept responsibility for the consequences. You aren't going to be cast out from a group of your true friends for making a mistake or embarrassing yourself. In fact, they will probably admire you even more for showing your human side.

Find Others Who Enjoy the Same Things You Do

One of the best ways to stop worrying about what others think about you is to surround yourself with people who enjoy the same things you do. Instead of faking the music you like, clothes you wear, or activities you love in order to fit in with a group that doesn't appreciate your interests, reach out to others who share your interests.

The people who want to know the real you often care about the same things you do. Not only will you be able to relax and be yourself in their presence, but they'll also provide support for your quest for self-love. In other words, they're your tribe. They're the people you can count on no matter what and who will continue to have your back even during the difficult times in your life.

With the availability of the Internet, you can find all sorts of groups and clubs that cater to every interest you can imagine. And if you can't, there's nothing that's stopping you from starting your own group. You are definitely not the only person who enjoys the things you do, but you have to be vulnerable and willing to show others who you really are so that you can find your tribe.

Others' Opinions Keep You Kind

One final thought on this subject. We should still use others' opinions to keep a check on our own behavior, especially when we're striving to become a kind and considerate person. When our behavior is too far out of whack, others will let us know. This is especially true for the people we have allowed to see our authentic selves. They care enough about us to tell us when we're acting out of character and we should use their opinions to correct our path.

This doesn't mean you are conforming to someone else's standards or trying to fit in by being something you're not. In fact, it's just the opposite. If you're being unkind, you're not fulfilling your quest for positive self-worth. You're trying to artificially and temporarily boost your self-esteem instead of building your value from the inside through kindness toward others.

CHAPTER THREE:
OUR VALUE IS MORE THAN OUR LOOKS

In an increasingly visual culture, the way our bodies look can become closely connected to how we feel about ourselves and our self-worth. As a society, we are moving away from being a better person and more toward looking like what we believe a good person should look like. Social media has done a great deal to contribute to this harmful phenomenon.

When survival depended on finding food, building shelter, and protecting themselves, people didn't care what they or others looked like as long as their bodies were functional and could do their part to ensure the community's survival. Everyone's bodies were designed to perform a necessary functions and appearances weren't on anyone's short list of concerns.

In those days, people weren't often exposed to people outside their own community, so they only saw people who looked like themselves. As time went on, though, through television primarily, people became inundated with images of other people, and in recent decades, those images have tended to be of thin people, especially thin women. Studies have shown that as people watched more television, they tended to want to change their bodies to look more like the images they saw on the screen.

Moreover, early television programs and magazines featured predominantly white characters and models, which contributed to a bias towards lighter skin. In fact, many people of color growing up in the early part of the 20th century never saw anyone like themselves on television or in magazines, something we know now to be extremely damaging to self-worth.

The image that slowly emerged to become the beauty standard we see all over the place today has expanded to include a specific look for each bodily feature. The nose must be small and upturned. The ears should be proportional to our head and not stick out. The chin should be square for men and round for women. The stomach should be flat and the skin should be tanned and free of blemishes. And on and on.

The tendency to feature characters and models who exemplified these arbitrary beauty standards became even more prevalent with the advent of fashion and entertainment magazines, and of course, the Internet. Combined with the relatively recent focus on the link between obesity and unhealthiness, society continues to promote an ideal body image standard that is impossible to attain and frequently dangerous to those who try.

WHERE WE DO IT

When we're young, we don't really see the physical differences in others. You can see this in the way that toddlers and preschoolers are friends with kids who are extremely different from them in appearance. Unfortunately, young people learn to judge as they get older, taking their cues from the not-so-subtle messages from various media and the people around them.

By the time kids enter middle school, they're already measuring themselves against the imaginary body image standards. They compare their bodies to what they see on television and in the movies. The heroes are almost always thin and beautiful, while the villains are often portrayed as the opposite. They are inundated with edited and filtered pictures on the Internet and in magazines. The people who are stereotypically beautiful get the most social media likes, shares, and followers.

At school, they see that the popular kids are often those who conform to society's beauty standard. While participating in a sport, they might be required to maintain a specific weight to be able to compete. At home, they may be told to watch what they eat or that they could stand to lose a few pounds. Or perhaps they see their parents struggle with their weight and understand that they're not happy with the way they look.

In other words, we begin believing our value is in how our body looks at a very young age and this message is everywhere, from the media we consume, to the comments we hear at school and home, to the advertising we are exposed to in nearly every public place. We really can't escape the pressure to look a certain way and along with that pressure comes a feeling of failure if we can't achieve it.

WHY WE DO IT

We Don't Want to Stand Out for Our Differences

The reason we associate our value with how we physically look is related to worrying about what others think of us. We want to belong. We don't want to stick out for any reason at all, and even though we can hide our thoughts, personality, and other parts of our nonphysical self, we simply can't hide our physical self. Therefore, we naturally want to do whatever we can to conform to society's standards of what an "acceptable" person looks like.

You probably already know that kids may find something to tease you about even if you don't have a feature that "sticks out." Kids can be cruel and they somehow have a radar for what we're most sensitive about. And if we get teased about something, we're more likely than ever to want to change it.

We're Constantly Told We Need to "Fix" Something

Of course, no one can achieve these impossibly high beauty standards, but that doesn't keep us from trying. Everywhere we turn, there's another article, television show, video, or comment that tells us we all have something we can "fix." We buy makeup to hide our flaws or make a specific feature that we like stand out. We go on crazy diets to lose weight. We seek out surgical and nonsurgical treatments to correct the imperfections that nature gave us.

In fact, the makeup and plastic surgery industries are huge businesses that are fueled by our desire to change something about ourselves that we think falls short of the beauty standard. These industries' entire business model depends on our insecurities about our bodies and, as a result, plastic surgery and makeup companies continue to promote this impossible standard and pressure people to conform to it.

Body Shaming is Rampant

And now, a new phenomenon has reared its ugly head in recent years that makes us feel even worse about our bodies if we aren't able to achieve the standard. Body shaming has been around for centuries, but with the proliferation of the Internet, it's never before been as rampant or as public as it is today. Body shaming is the practice of criticizing another person based on a physical characteristic and it's extremely harmful to individuals' sense of self-worth.

Some people believe that by criticizing someone about their body, particularly their weight, it will cause them to make lifestyle changes that will get them closer to society's beauty standard. What they don't understand is that by body shaming someone, they're saying that the person is worth less than someone else who better represents the ideal body image. This is absolutely untrue, but unless we know how to combat body shaming, we can internalize those comments and allow them to negatively impact our self-worth.

Other people body shame because of that brief flash of self-esteem they get from momentarily feeling like they're superior to someone else. Again, just as with other types of negative comments, their critique of someone else's body is a reflection of how they feel about themselves, but they get a boost in self-esteem by putting another person down.

This, of course, does nothing to help their own self-worth, but in the moment, they don't realize that their comments are as harmful to them as they are to the person they're directed at. They are ashamed of something about themselves (their own body shape or weight, a particular feature, etc.), but they don't know how to deal with that shame so they settle for that self-esteem boost.

Recently, there have been attempts to promote body positivity and to combat body shaming. This is an excellent step forward, but the concept of a perfect body is so ingrained in our society that it's going to take a monumental effort to turn the tide the other way. Fortunately, there are ways to tackle the problem of viewing your body as your value on an individual level, which is where true change must begin.

WHY WE SHOULDN'T DO IT

We shouldn't place our value as a human being on the way our body looks because that isn't a true source of value. Your value has absolutely nothing to do with your appearance, despite all the messages you receive that tell you otherwise. Your value is in your personality, actions, and beliefs and it doesn't matter what packaging those character traits come in. What matters is the kind of person you are.

Everyone Dislikes Some Things about Their Body

You already know that nobody's perfect and that extends to our bodies as well. Everyone has something they don't like about themselves. They might think their ears aren't symmetrical or that they'd rather have blue eyes instead of brown. They might hate their hair because it's difficult to style or they wish their teeth were straight.

We must keep in mind that just because we don't like something about ourselves doesn't mean we have to change it. Of course, you can change it if you want to, but you shouldn't do it because you're trying to measure up to an arbitrary standard. You should only do it if it contributes to your journey toward self-love.

Everyone Has Things about Their Body They Like

Conversely, everyone has something about their body that they love. Often, it's a feature that other people tell us is attractive and it often matches a part of the ideal beauty image, but by focusing on the things we like about our bodies, we can become less preoccupied with what we find less desirable.

Beauty Comes in All Forms

The point here is that beauty comes in all forms. Society's ideal beauty standards are completely arbitrary. At one point, they were a single person's perception of what is beautiful and because that one person had access to technology and the ability to put those standards in front of people, their perception became everyone's reality.

Just as every person prefers a different style of art, every person has a different idea of what constitutes beauty. The challenge is in learning to override what others tell us is beautiful to discover what we really believe to be beautiful ourselves. We have to practice finding our own aesthetic so we can appreciate beauty in all its various forms.

The World Would Be Boring if Everyone was the Same

Inherently, standards are designed to give everyone a blueprint of what is "correct"; whether it's a manufacturing standard or an academic standard, the idea behind it is to make something the same. But what would the world be like if everyone looked the same? It wouldn't be very interesting, that's for sure. Yet, that's what millions of people strive for every time they change something about themselves in an attempt to reach society's beauty standard.

True Beauty Lies in Self-Acceptance

Ultimately, the most beautiful people are those who are their true selves. They love themselves and they are more concerned with being a good person than they are with what they look like. Getting to this point is difficult, but it can be done, as previously mentioned, with a shift in focus and perspective and a lot of practice.

HOW TO
STOP DOING IT

Research shows that 86% of women and girls are dissatisfied with their bodies and view their body as a definitive element of their identities. This is massive and extremely hard to change. Learning at a young age that you are so much more than your body size, shape, or color is vital to shifting the societal narrative around body image. That's part of what this guide aims to do, but individuals like you have to do the work.

Focus on What You Love about Your Body

The first step toward altering your perspective is to alter your focus. Instead of obsessing about the things you dislike about your body, place your focus on what you do like. At first, this might seem difficult because we're socialized to pay attention to what society views as our flaws. You might have to start small, but it only matters that you start.

For instance, if you like the color of your eyes, say that out loud: "My eyes are a very pretty shade of green." Saying it out loud makes it real and your brain will process it as a compliment, releasing those feel-good endorphins that boost your mood. When you repeat them regularly, you're embedding these positive comments in your subconscious.

Try to choose five things you like about your body and say them out loud several times a day. After you do this for a few days or weeks, you will find other things about your body that you appreciate. Add these to your affirmations and continue to build your list as you find more positive things to notice about your body.

Intentionally Stop Making Body Comparisons

We've already addressed comparing yourself to others in a previous section of this guide, but it's essential to stop comparing your body with other people in order to move beyond viewing your body as your value. Remember that no two bodies are the same and they shouldn't be. If we were all intended to look alike, we would have been born that way.

Comparing your body to someone else's is not helpful because while you might be able to control some aspects of your appearance, there is so much beyond your control that it's literally impossible to become exactly like another person. You can't control your height, hair type, skin color, skin type, and much more.

What's more is that it can be dangerous for you to try to change your body to match what you see as the ideal body image. Such comparisons can lead to eating disorders or obsessive dieting that leave you malnourished and weak. At worst, these conditions can be fatal.

Rather than comparing your body to someone else's, try setting personal goals that keep your body healthy. Don't focus on the number on the scale or the size of clothes you wear. Instead, work on making yourself feel good and strong. Eat as well as you can, exercise within your limits, and take good care of your skin, especially when you're outside. When you feel good physically, you'll be less likely to compare yourself to others.

Focus on How Your Body Serves You in Its Present Form

Your body was designed to allow you to function throughout life. When you focus on function instead of appearance, you can start to appreciate what you are able to do with your body. For example, maybe you've been told you have large shoulders, something that society doesn't view as "feminine." However, those shoulders might make you one heck of a swimmer or gymnast.

Perhaps someone has criticized your thick thighs (a common criticism for women), but did you know that scientists have linked thick thighs with a lower risk for heart disease? So, you actually might be healthier with your thick thighs than someone who has that thigh gap that's nearly impossible to achieve. Plus, larger thighs are also important for athletes in numerous sports like soccer, sprinting, basketball, and tennis, so they don't get injured and can power through their competitions.

It's also interesting to note that bodybuilders often have a physique that's admired by millions of people who wish they could have a "six pack" or bulging biceps. But many of those same bodybuilders can't even bend over to tie their shoes because they're "muscle bound," a condition that results in muscles that have little to no elasticity because they're overworked. Maybe you don't look as defined as a bodybuilder, but wouldn't you rather be able to tie your own shoes? Give your body credit for being able to do everyday tasks that we often take for granted.

Change the Things You Can (But Only If You Want To)

We live in a world where nearly every physical feature can be altered to better align with society's ideal body image. You can get a rhinoplasty to change the shape and size of your nose. You can have your ears pinned so they don't stick out as far. You can enlarge certain body parts and diminish others. There are even treatments to lighten or darken your skin, reduce the appearance of scars, remove hair, and more.

This guide isn't going to tell you not to undergo procedures or treatments to change things about yourself that you don't like. After all, the technology exists and if you believe a treatment will help you love yourself more, you should explore the options. But you should only make changes for yourself and not for anyone else. Many of these treatments and procedures are very expensive and some are painful and carry risks, so they should not be undertaken lightly.

Most of the time, you'll have to be an adult before you can undergo elective surgeries and treatments, or you'll be required to have a parent's approval. There are good reasons for this, one of which is that as you mature, you're more likely to appreciate your unique body and its features, especially if you practice self-love and separate your body from your self-worth.

It's easier said than done, but if you can move toward loving yourself instead of looking for external validation, you won't need to change much, if anything, about the way you look. You'll love yourself for who you are, and that is what true beauty is all about.

Practice Mindfulness

Mindfulness is the act of being aware and present at any given moment and it can really help you focus on what your body can do instead of how it looks. Throughout the day, try to notice when you are comparing your body to someone else's and when you're criticizing something you don't like about your body. Actively explore the feelings you're having at these times, even if they're painful.

When you notice yourself comparing your body or criticizing your appearance, stop and replace those thoughts with positive ones. Instead of saying, "I wish my stomach was flat like Leah's," say, "I feel strong and confident in my body," or "I love the color of my eyes because they make me feel unique and special." Again, say these things out loud in the moment so you can shift your thinking from negative to positive.

Keep in mind that your body is a process, not a product. This means that it's always changing, from birth until old age. Your goal is to accept its present form at any stage and know that it's going to change again. What matters is that it's still functional and that you're still able to do the things you want to do in the body you have.

Fight Your Own Tendencies to Body Shame

The urge to comment on other people's bodies is ingrained in us from an early age. But, to really turn the tide toward body acceptance, we have to fight our own tendencies to body shame others. Just as you tell yourself that your body is fine in whatever shape or size it is, the same is true for everyone.

Make a list of people you admire who don't have the "ideal" body and write down what you admire about them. You'll see that these people are not valued because of what they look like, but rather for who they are. It's also beneficial to know that today's ideal body image hasn't been around that long. The people considered most beautiful a century ago probably wouldn't be admired today, as society's beauty standards are constantly changing. All the more reason not to measure yourself against them.

Once you get better at fighting your own body shaming tendencies, you'll be able to recognize when others are doing the same, and you'll be able to call them out for it by explaining how their observations are hurting people. This doesn't mean you have to be on a one-person crusade to stop body shaming, but you can make a difference by educating others about this harmful practice.

CHAPTER FOUR:
LETTING GO OF TOXIC PEOPLE

There are some people who seem to live expressly to make other people feel bad about themselves. Whether they're always putting others down or they're more subtle and give backhanded compliments that send the message that they're better than others, these people can be a big part of why girls have trouble loving themselves.

Sometimes, we know we should put distance between ourselves and the people who make us feel worthless, but for some reason, we aren't able to do it. Instead, we let them chip away at our self-worth and derail our efforts to become the person we want to be. Other times, we don't even realize that someone is a toxic force in our lives because they're people who are supposed to love us and we aren't able to get away from them.

When you're young, you may not be able to completely cut out some of the people who add toxicity to your life, but you can limit your interaction with them as much as possible until you're old enough to make those decisions yourself. However, if the toxic people are your "friends," you absolutely can and should stop hanging on to them.

WHERE WE DO IT

Toxic people are everywhere, and when you're young, you're likely to encounter them at school and online. Certainly, there might be some family members who contribute to negativity in your life, but usually family members want the best for you and are willing to do whatever they can to help you have a high sense of self-worth. If there is a family member who is causing you to feel badly, talk to your parents and let them know your feelings. They are there to help.

At school, it can be difficult to get away from bullies or "friends" who are anything but friendly. It gets better as you get older and you're not all in the same classes together, but there are still times when you'll come into contact with people who are intent on tearing you down. This can also happen in various other places such as church or work, but you spend so much time in school that it is almost inevitably the place where you'll face many of your day-to-day struggles.

You'll also encounter toxic people online, especially because people can hide behind their computer screens and say things to others that they would never say to them in person. While the actual act of blocking these people online is simple, letting them go is not always easy, particularly if they pretend to be your friend when they really aren't.

When you're trying to be a kind person, cutting toxic people out of your life might seem counter to that goal. But remember that you must be kind to yourself first and if there are people at school, online, at church, work, or anywhere else who are not allowing you to be kind to yourself, you need to protect yourself from them.

WHY WE DO IT

The main reason why we hang on to toxic people is once again rooted in our ancestry. When our daily lives were filled with obstacles that had to be overcome for survival, we needed everyone to work together to achieve that goal. Those who didn't actively work in the group didn't survive. Now, thousands of years later, we still fear letting go of anyone, even though we no longer need everyone for survival.

We Don't Like Conflict

Most of us don't want conflict in our lives, so we would rather not rock the boat by severing a toxic relationship. We tell ourselves that we can handle their negativity and that the positive aspects of your friendship usually outweighs the negatives anyway. But, when you rationalize holding onto a toxic person, you're allowing them to continue treating you poorly, even if it doesn't happen often.

We Fear Letting Go

You might even fear that if you drop this friendship that you won't have other friends, so you'd rather hang on to the one you have, even if it's not good for you. Again, this fear is related to our social nature. We do not want to be alone and we'll tell ourselves that it's better to have a toxic friend in our lives than no friends at all.

Of course, it's not true that you won't have other friends in your life if you let a toxic friend go, but sometimes you can't see that until the toxic person is gone. Negative people tend to be a major force in our lives, so much so that we can't see what else is out there for us. You might even discover that people wanted to be your friend all along, but couldn't get past the toxic person to get to know you.

We Don't Like Change

Many humans are also change averse, meaning they don't like change. They like routine and consistency, and removing a toxic person from their lives can be a huge change. Sometimes, we just want things to stay the way they are because we don't want to go through the tough times that change brings, so we choose to keep things as they are. This also benefits the toxic person, though, because they don't want to change, either.

We Think We Deserve Toxicity

Another reason we might hang onto a toxic person in our lives is because we think we deserve it. Until we begin to love ourselves, we might believe that the things they say and do to us are for our own good. For instance, if a "friend" is always telling you that you'll never have a boyfriend if you don't dress differently, you might think they're helping you instead of putting you down for the way you like to dress.

Toxicity can sometimes be subtle and we might not even recognize it until the damage is done. For example, someone who is always involved in drama is probably toxic. They like being in the middle of conflict and will often inflame emotions just to see what happens. In other words, they learn what buttons to push and then proceed to push them for their own entertainment. Even if you're not the focus of the drama (this time), be aware that someone who drama seems to follow could turn on you at any time.

We Blame Ourselves for How Others Treat Us

Self-blame is another reason we tend to hold onto toxic people. We think that the person wouldn't be putting us down or treating us poorly if we were a better person ourselves. Of course, this isn't true at all. When someone treats you poorly, it's a reflection of their own self-hate and they're trying to make themselves feel better by making you feel worse. It usually only works for a few seconds, but that boost to their self-esteem is addicting, so they keep doing it.

Your own actions very rarely have anything to do with why someone continually treats you poorly. You won't make them treat you better by being kinder or spending money on them or doing things for them. In fact, they might even treat you worse because they see you respond by blaming yourself and doubling down on your efforts to please them.

WHY WE SHOULDN'T DO IT

They Make Us Feel Bad about Ourselves

The most obvious reason why we shouldn't keep toxic people in our lives if we can help it is because they make us feel bad about ourselves. We are already battling constant messages we can't control that say we're not good enough. Why should we allow something we can control to do the same thing? The answer is that we shouldn't.

If you feel bad about yourself after engaging with a supposed "friend," relative, or anyone else, it's time to reevaluate your relationship with that person. The people in your life should lift you up and make you feel good about yourself and what you offer to the world. People who put you down or let you down with their words or actions aren't moving you toward your goal of self-love. They're actively blocking you from loving yourself.

They Cause Us Pain

They are also causing you pain, if not physically, then emotionally. You don't deserve to hurt all the time because someone is treating you poorly. And even if letting a toxic person go is somewhat painful, it's better to suffer that temporary pain than to continue to expose yourself to hurt whenever you're around that person.

Plus, it's a different type of pain because when you let someone go who's causing you pain, you know that you're doing it to give yourself peace. When someone is hurting you through their actions and words, the pain is internalized, where it damages your self-worth.

They Are Exhausting

Toxic people also take a lot of energy to be around, usually on your part. You may worry about saying or doing the wrong thing that might anger them or you may be constantly looking for ways to make them happy. These are very time-consuming and energy-depleting actions that might not even work in the first place. You want friends who are happy just to be your friend and who don't expect anything else from you. These are people who are easy to be around because you can let down your guard and be yourself, which is the easiest person for you to be, after all.

They Hold Us Back

Whether you realize it or not, the toxic people in your life are holding you back. They are preventing you from being your authentic self because they're making you doubt yourself and your strengths. They might make you feel insignificant or think that your ideas are unimportant, especially if they ignore your contributions or treat you like your opinions don't matter.

You want people in your life who help you progress toward your goals, who support you through the good times and the bad, and who value your ideas and opinions. Fortunately, there are more of these people in your life than toxic people, but sometimes, the toxic people take up a lot of the room and air in your space so that they are all you see and hear. When they're finally not there, you'll be amazed at how much you grow!

HOW TO
STOP DOING IT

You may not be able to fully relieve yourself of all the toxic people in your life, especially if some of them are family members. It's an unfortunate truth that sometimes people in our families are not always good for us. But, in most cases, our families want us to be our best selves and will do what they can to help us.

Siblings can be especially challenging if they're around the same age as you because they're going through many of the same things. They're trying to learn how to love themselves and may be lost or confused throughout that process. If possible, share some things you've learned about self-love to give them some ideas about their own journey and that may be enough to change their behavior. Chances are your siblings *aren't* toxic. They're just searching for themselves.

Likewise, friends your age may also not necessarily be toxic, even if they're treating you poorly. The difference is that you don't have to live with your friends, so you can take action to limit your exposure to their toxicity. And that leads us to our first tip.

Limit Contact with Them

It may be too much for you to cut toxic people out of your life entirely, especially if you're still learning who those people are. You don't have to completely stop hanging on to people who may be toxic, but you should limit contact with them. Instead of spending time outside of school with that "friend" who's always causing drama, try only seeing them at school and in the classes you have together. You don't even have to have lunch with them or spend your breaks with them. Limit your contact to school-related activities such as assignments and sports.

They might ask you why you're not hanging out with them anymore, but you don't owe them an explanation. You can just say you're busy or that you're focusing on yourself for a while. You might tell them that you don't feel good about yourself when you're around them, but if you think they might get angry or upset, there's no need to go into detail.

However, letting them know that you're not going to accept their treatment of you anymore may be what they need to hear. Toxic people aren't known for their reflection and introspection, but if they don't know they've hurt you, they don't have an opportunity to change. If you want to give them that chance and you feel comfortable doing so, talking with the person about why you're distancing yourself from them could be worthwhile.

Set Boundaries

If you're not ready to limit contact with someone in your life quite yet, you can continue your relationship with them as long as they respect your boundaries. Boundaries can be anything you need to protect yourself and prevent a toxic person from making you feel bad about yourself. For example, a boundary you might set is "When you make a joke about me in front of our friends, it makes me feel bad and I would like you to stop."

The key to setting boundaries is to communicate them clearly to the other person so they know which behaviors will cross the boundaries. Toxic people aren't always good with boundaries though, and they may push back or continue to violate your boundaries even if you're absolutely clear about them. If this happens, you will need to limit contact with that person, which is a natural consequence of them crossing your line.

Other boundaries might include turning off your phone when you don't want to speak to the person, limiting how much you see of the person on social media, leaving the situation if the person continues a behavior after you've asked them to stop, not participating in any drama that surrounds that person (whether it involves you or not), and asking for help from adults if a negative behavior doesn't stop.

A final point on boundaries: You have to follow through with your boundaries with toxic people. They often attempt to manipulate you or play on your compassion to cross them, but until they respect your line in the sand, you can't fulfill your self-love journey. Their behavior will continue to bring you down and prevent you from being who you are meant to be. Sometimes, the only option is to cut a person out of your life for good, especially if they continue to disregard your feelings and overstep your boundaries.

Block Them on Social Media (or at Least Set Limits)

As briefly mentioned earlier, toxic people thrive online. Their filters seem to drop, allowing them to say things they would never say in person. Unfortunately, one bad comment online can make you forget about all the positive experiences you've had on various Internet platforms. This is due to what scientists call "negativity bias," which means humans have a tendency to dwell on the negative rather than the positive.

In fact, negativity bias is often responsible for our own self-criticism as well. We think something negative about ourselves and that negativity multiplies until we're drowning in it. It takes many more positive thoughts to cancel out a single negative one, both in our heads and online.

Someone who might be perfectly nice and seemingly kind in person can turn into a toxic element when they're behind a screen and unable to see the person they're putting down. They may not even fully understand how their words are affecting you and it's possible they don't intend to hurt you or anyone else.

But if they're made aware of how their online actions are impacting you, and their behavior doesn't change, you have tools available to you to take control over who you interact with online. Nearly all social media platforms and texting applications, for instance, allow you to block users so they can't contact you. This might seem extreme, but even if you only block them for a while, you are taking steps to protect your emotional well-being.

In some cases, a toxic person might not be communicating with you directly, but their posts might be causing you stress, anxiety, or other negative feelings. For example, they might be posting about the most recent drama they're involved in and you don't want to participate (good for you!). There are tools that can limit what you see from that person or you can "snooze" them for a period of time if you just need a break.

No one has the right to take away your inner peace, so if someone is doing that through their online actions, you need to take the steps to remove yourself from that situation. You're not forced to be on social media and if it's doing you more harm than good, it might be time to limit how much time you spend on these platforms or really restrict what you see and do while you're online.

Spend Time with Positive People

Once again, if a toxic person is around you, they're probably taking up a lot of your time and space. It can be difficult to see that most people in your life are positive and good for your well-being. Once you get away from the toxic person for a bit and you start spending time with these positive people, you'll realize that your true friends make you feel good about yourself. They celebrate who you are and feed your self-worth, and you do the same for them.

Science has proven that emotions are contagious. When you're around someone who is positive, you'll feel more positive, too. Their glass-half-full approach to life will also make you feel more hopeful and motivated to reach your goals. They don't get drawn into drama because they refuse to put themselves in negative situations and instead are concerned about living in the moment.

Positive people also give excellent advice because they're interested in helping you live your best life. They don't want to hold you back to make themselves look better. Instead, they will guide you to make better decisions that will enrich your experiences. And you'll just be happier, mostly because when you spend time with positive people, your focus will be on more positive things.

You'll discover that when you surround yourself with positive people, you'll wonder why you ever let a negative person drag you down. You'll begin to recognize toxicity earlier and be able to either set boundaries sooner or distance yourself from their negativity. And you'll be drawn back to your positive circle and want to remain there because it feels so good.

Don't Get Drawn into Drama

Toxic people thrive on drama and they want to drag everyone else into their theatrical productions. They like to push buttons to see how far they can go before the other person gets angry or upset. Often, they start the drama only to sit back and let other people entertain them as they fight or argue. Toxic people are good at getting others to participate in their drama by making everything an "us versus them" situation.

One of the best things you can do to get toxic people out of your life is to refuse to be drawn into their drama. This is challenging because middle school and high school are prime dramatic years anyway, but it's also the perfect time for you to develop a reputation for not getting involved in or perpetuating drama.

Learn to recognize when a person is going to start drama. They might begin gossiping about other people or confront someone they have a problem with (possibly even you). The keys to avoiding drama are to remain calm, set boundaries, and if all else fails, walk away. When you remain calm, you aren't giving the person the reaction they want. And when they start drama, they are doing it for the reaction.

Often, the situation can be diffused pretty quickly if no one reacts, because what fun is drama if there isn't any actual drama? You should also set boundaries right from the start. If someone starts gossiping about another person, for example, ask them to stop.

If they don't, or they continue to escalate a situation, then physically remove yourself by walking away. Toxic people want an audience for their drama, and even if others are willing to give them what they want, you shouldn't for your own well-being.

Online drama is also toxic, but it's easier not to get drawn into it if you're willing to do what it takes to avoid it. Don't respond to inflammatory comments and don't insert yourself into an argument that doesn't involve you. If someone else is getting bullied or is otherwise in danger, report the behavior to an adult, but refrain from taking part. Use blocking and post-limiting tools to remove the temptation to participate and get off social media altogether if it's making you feel anxious or stressed.

Forgive Them, but Don't Forget

Forgiving someone doesn't mean they weren't wrong and it doesn't give them a pass to treat you poorly. All it does is free you from the hold they have over you. It's not even necessary for you to forgive the person by telling them you forgive them. You just have to forgive them in your heart so you can move on.

When you forgive a toxic person for hurting you, it doesn't mean you have to go back to being their friend or allow them back into your life without boundaries. It just means that you have changed the way you're viewing the situation so that you can work on improving yourself. Not everyone needs to forgive the people who have hurt them, but for many people, it gives them permission to let go of the pain they endured.

Whether you choose to forgive someone in person or just in your own heart, don't forget how they treated you and why you took steps to distance yourself from them. You don't have to let them back into your life unless you want to and have a healthy way to allow them back in; and you don't have to give them another chance, especially if you've given them numerous chances before.

Forgiveness is for you and not them. It's giving you the space to enjoy the good memories you have with the person so you can let go of any lingering emotional energy they're taking up inside you. This way, you can focus your energy on positive actions that move you toward your goal of self-love.

CHAPTER FIVE:

DOUBTING OURSELVES

We aren't born with self-doubt. When we're born and as we grow into toddlers and preschoolers, we think we can do anything. We definitely try to do everything, because that's how we learn about the world around us. We only start to doubt ourselves when we fail at something we really want to do and when we're exposed to the limits society and other people attempt to place on us.

Self-doubt usually rears its head whenever we're doing something we deem worthwhile. We question our abilities and think of all the things that could go wrong. Again, it's human nature to dwell on the negative (remember negativity bias), but if you doubt yourself at every turn, it's going to limit your accomplishments and contribute to negative feelings toward your self-worth.

When we doubt ourselves, we can spiral into thinking that nothing we do is good enough and that we'll never amount to anything. Even worse is if we hear others say we can't do something or that we're not good at something. We internalize criticism (even constructive criticism) and often allow it to turn into self-doubt. Self-doubt is an obstacle to self-love, so we have to learn how to stop doubting our abilities and regain the confidence we had when we were little.

WHERE WE DO IT

The primary place where girls experience self-doubt is in school. Studies have shown that girls start to think they're less intelligent than boys by age six, which is right about when they enter school. More research is needed to understand the dynamics that go into why girls begin to doubt their own abilities, but it's thought to be related to subconscious societal biases.

Even though girls generally out-perform boys in school, especially at the elementary levels, there is a large gender gap in STEM (science, technology, engineering, and math) fields. Traditionally, girls were steered away from careers in these fields, while boys were encouraged to pursue them. In recent decades, there have been improvements in closing this gap, but it's still present.

Girls are also genetically predisposed to be more careful and take less risks than boys are; boys' testosterone levels increase risk-taking behaviors and boost self-confidence levels. Additionally, boys are often raised to have a tougher attitude than girls, who are often raised to be gentle and caring. These factors lead men to potentially be more resilient than women, who tend to take setbacks harder.

Self-doubt in school can lead girls to take classes that they know they will succeed in and avoid classes that they might struggle in. As a result, they will usually gravitate toward jobs that might not challenge or fulfill them. And when faced with some decisions, self-doubt can creep in, making them question their choices and obsess about potential failures. Even if those failures never come to pass, self-doubt about that possibility increases anxiety and stress levels.

Girls also experience self-doubt when they're with their friends and are presented with unhealthy situations. If they aren't confident in making the right choice, they are more likely to give into the pressure to do dangerous things. They may not believe they are capable of making a good choice, so they allow their peers to make those choices for them. Additionally, the fear of speaking up and being criticized for that can prevent them from making a choice they know is right.

WHY WE DO IT

We Fear Making Mistakes and We Dwell on Them

Doubting ourselves comes back to wanting to belong. We are afraid of making mistakes and embarrassing ourselves in front of others. We internalize the mistakes we've made in the past and instead of viewing those mistakes as learning opportunities, we use them as reminders of what happened the last time we made a mistake. In essence, we are learning from our mistakes, but we're learning the wrong lesson.

We Want to Be Perfect

We logically know that no one is perfect, but again, as with worrying about what people think about us, we want to be perfect so that we're accepted. Of course, making mistakes doesn't make you less worthy of acceptance, but we let our fear of embarrassment and criticism from others block that reality. We assign worthiness to how perfect we can be instead of understanding that mistakes are leading us to the person we ultimately want to be.

We Worry About What Can Go Wrong

Girls in particular may worry about what will go wrong if they make a certain choice instead of what can go right. They often over-analyze a situation by considering the consequences of each action. Certainly, thinking about the consequences before making a decision is a good practice, but not if it paralyzes you from making that decision or inserts doubt where there shouldn't be any.

For example, pretend there is a story writing contest at school. You have received high marks in your English classes for your writing and you really enjoy it, but you want to think about what could happen if you do enter. Those without self-doubt will think about the positive consequences: the judges love your story, you win the contest, and you receive positive comments about your story that will help you write even better.

Those with self-doubt, though, automatically jump to potential negative consequences: the judges hate your story. They laugh at your skills. You don't win and you receive criticism about your story that indicates you shouldn't be a writer at all. The result? You don't enter the contest or you seek reassurance and validation from other people to help you make your decision.

You might ask your teachers and friends if you should enter your story because you need to hear them say you're a good writer and have a chance to win. Instead of telling yourself that, you're relying on other people's opinions to make your decision. This does nothing to alleviate your self-doubt and in fact makes you doubt yourself even more because you may think you can't make decisions on your own.

We Don't Trust Our Instincts

In most cases, your instincts are right and will guide you to the right decision without the need for external validation. You know you've received high marks in English and you know you're a good writer. Your instincts are telling you that entering the contest is the right decision, but your fear of criticism and rejection are pushing your instincts out of the way to make room for self-doubt.

This is especially an issue if your instincts have steered you wrong before. You may begin to not trust them even though your intuition is almost always valid and worth listening to. Our worries about what can go wrong and our fear of criticism can override our instincts no matter how insistent they are.

WHY WE SHOULDN'T DO IT

Self-doubt, mistakes, and fear are intertwined, making it difficult to extricate one from the others. To minimize self-doubt, we have to accept that we will make mistakes and we have to get over our fears of criticism, failure, and rejection. This is no easy task, especially the longer we have allowed those negative thoughts to fester in our brain.

Mistakes Are Necessary for Self-Improvement

We need mistakes in our lives so we can improve. Without mistakes, we are stuck in place rather than moving toward the life we want. Not only do mistakes and failures show us where we went wrong and give us ideas of how to do better next time, but they also make success taste so much sweeter! In fact, without mistakes, we would just come to accept success as something that happens to us instead of something we achieve through hard work and determination.

We Are Reluctant to Try New Things

Moreover, self-doubt keeps us from trying new things that could turn out to be incredible experiences. When we worry about the bad things that could happen, we talk ourselves out of taking risks. We might never try that new sport that looks like fun and therefore, we don't know if we might be so good at that sport that it becomes our passion. We might never get our driver's license, so we don't make that road trip after graduation that leads us to the perfect place to live.

As we get older, we might not go for that promotion at work or accept a date from someone who we find intriguing. We might not write that novel we've always wanted to write or try for that internship that could lead to our ideal job.

Sure, it's safer not to take risks. You won't get rejected and you won't fail, but you're also removing possibilities from your life. Self-doubt keeps you where you are and doesn't allow you to grow into the person you're supposed to be.

And as we get older, we become less willing to take these risks because we've accumulated more years of self-doubt. We think we're too old to change careers or get a degree. We think our best years are behind us so why bother learning new things? The earlier you can cast out self-doubt, the more fulfilling your life will be because you won't place limits on yourself.

It's Unhealthy — Both Physically and Mentally

Ultimately, self-doubt increases our stress levels, which can lead to all sorts of health problems. We may not get enough sleep because we're worrying about our decisions. We're second-guessing our choices and stressing out about the potential problems that can arise. A lack of sleep is linked to a wide range of physical ailments including high blood pressure, diabetes, heart disease, obesity, depression, and more. So, learning to minimize self-doubt will make you healthier, both physically and mentally.

In addition, when we are confident and trust our instincts, we tend to make better and healthier decisions. Remember that peer pressure thing? When we trust our intuition that following the crowd might be dangerous, we are more likely to choose not to give in to peer pressure, which is usually the healthier choice. And, knowing that we made the right choice will allow us to sleep better as well.

HOW TO
STOP DOING IT

So, how do we learn how to trust ourselves again after we've already allowed self-doubt to take hold? It's not going to be easy and will require lots of practice, but it can be done. Note that some amount of self-doubt is always going to creep into your mind because that's how we can tell when something's meaningful to us. We rarely doubt ourselves when our decisions don't really matter.

For example, you probably don't second-guess your choice of socks to wear to school because in the long run, it really doesn't matter. But you might doubt your decision to try out for the basketball team because making the team is something you really want. When we care about how our decisions impact our lives, we tend to have more self-doubt. It's only natural, but it's what you do about that self-doubt that matters.

Trust Your Instincts

Combating self-doubt requires trusting yourself and your decisions. You have instincts for a reason and they're well-founded in your life experiences. Listen to what they're telling you and trust your inner voice to tell you what to do. If your intuition is telling you something is a bad idea, it probably is. On the other hand, if it's telling you to go for it, there might be a good reason for that.

Now, your instincts aren't always right, so trusting them doesn't mean you won't make a mistake or that failure won't follow. These are always possibilities, but your instincts are right more often than not and they'll only get stronger as you follow them. Regaining your trust takes time, just as it would if you needed to regain another person's trust and it starts by listening to yourself.

Avoid Seeking Validation from External Sources

You'll also want to avoid seeking reassurance and validation whenever possible, especially if you already know the right choice. External validation does nothing to decrease self-doubt because it only reinforces the idea that you can't make your own decisions.

Of course, if you need advice to help you make a decision, you should talk to others and get their opinions, especially if you aren't sure of the consequences of making a specific choice. You are still young and you might need others' experience to give you enough information to make a decision. This is not undermining your instincts at all, but is instead ensuring you have all the available information you need to give those instincts a chance to guide you.

When seeking advice about a situation, make sure to get it from people who have your best interests at heart. Keep toxic people in mind so that they don't sabotage your efforts and don't seek out opinions from strangers online as they don't know enough about you to give sound advice. They could lead your instincts astray by providing suggestions that are the opposite of what you really need, particularly if you leave out any pertinent facts (a tendency that we have when we want strangers to validate the decision we want to make).

Use Positive Visualization

Instead of focusing on the potential negative consequences of a decision, try using positive visualization to imagine what will happen if things go right. Elite athletes use this technique all the time to help them achieve their in-game goals.

For instance, a kicker in football will visualize his kick going through the goalposts before he actually makes the attempt. When you focus on the positive outcomes of a situation, your brain already thinks you've achieved your goal so the actual act of achieving it is just a formality.

Certainly, this doesn't work 100% of the time, but studies have shown that thinking positively increases your focus on success, which in turn makes you work harder to actually achieve it. Even if you don't succeed the first time, positive visualization can give you the motivation to keep pursuing success. In other words, it reduces your self-doubt because you can see yourself achieving your goal in your mind so you know you can do it.

Set Reasonable Goals

When it comes to setting goals, there are many different ways to go about identifying and articulating which goals you will set, and then how you'll go about accomplishing them. One strategy is to set SMART goals. SMART is an acronym to describe effective goals, in which S = Specific; M = Measurable; A = Attainable; R = Realistic; and T = Timely. So, "smart" goals are specific, measurable, attainable, realistic, and timely goals.

When you set goals that you can actually achieve, and give yourself a timeframe in which to do so, you're setting yourself up for success. And every time you reach an attainable goal, you're edging self-doubt out of your mind and increasing your confidence and self-trust.

Good goals should stretch your abilities a little bit, but they should still be in range for you to reach in a relatively short amount of time. As such, even though you might have big dreams, your SMART goals should be the smaller steps it will take to reach your ultimate dream.

Breaking up long-term goals into several short-term goals is vital for you to feel like you're making progress. This also allows you to celebrate small accomplishments along the way, something that is necessary for driving out self-doubt. At first, make your SMART goals as small as you need to begin trusting yourself again, but over time, start setting slightly bigger goals that are still attainable, exercising your self-trust muscle.

Be Decisive

Boys are often viewed as more decisive than girls because when they see something they want, they typically go for it. Girls, on the other hand, tend to analyze the entire situation, consider the consequences, and get input on what they should do. Of course, this isn't true for every girl, just as risk-taking isn't a characteristic of every boy. But these stereotypes exist for a reason: there's some truth to them.

Decisiveness is a potent tool for banishing self-doubt because once you've made a decision, you often can't change your mind. You can't start thinking about everything that could go wrong and ignoring your instincts because you've already made your choice. This doesn't mean every single decision you make will have only positive results, but it does mean you'll have less time to stress about potential negative outcomes.

The only caveat with being decisive is that even after you make a decision, you can be inundated with "what if?" worries. The key to keeping these thoughts at bay is to remind yourself that what's done is done. In many instances, it's difficult to change the decision you've made, so you have to see it through. When you tell your brain that it's doing you no good to obsess over something that can't be changed, you'll be able to turn your thoughts to something else.

Practice Mindfulness

Speaking of turning your thoughts to something else, another thing you can do to stop doubting yourself is to practice mindfulness. When you actively consider your thoughts and feelings in the moment, you can control what you're thinking about and feeling. Just as you can force your brain to stop obsessing about things it can't control, you can force your brain to stop doubting yourself.

When you start to wonder if you are capable of doing something, or you're hesitant to try something new because you don't know if you'll be good at it, stop and explore those thoughts and ask yourself what you're feeling. Are you worried about failure? If so, why? What is the worst thing that could happen if you fail? Are you concerned you don't have the skills? If so, remind yourself of the skills you do have and align them to the situation at hand.

This is the perfect time to also practice positive visualization so you can shift your perspective away from doubt and toward confidence. What would success look like? How are you going to feel when you achieve this goal? What will people say about you when you succeed? Positive visualization is an excellent mindfulness technique that keeps you focused on the good outcomes instead of obsessing over potential bad results.

Make Mistakes

Yes, you must make mistakes. This is because mistakes teach us what doesn't work and opens our minds to new possibilities and creative thinking. You might have heard the expression that you learn more from your failures than you do from your successes, and this is absolutely true. Your failures are lessons that you take with you the next time you try something and inspire you to do better.

Mistakes also free us from fear because when the worst happens and we don't succeed, we realize that the outcome is not as bad as we worried it might be. Failure is a major fear, but that's because we strive for perfection and don't want to embarrass ourselves by proving to be less than perfect. But, when we actually fail, we discover that it's not as big of a deal as we made it out to be. The world doesn't stop, people move on, and we try again.

If you aren't making mistakes, you aren't taking risks, which means you're doubting yourself. You believe the chance of failure is so high that it's better to not try at all. But by reframing failure as a necessary component of growth instead of something to avoid, you can overcome your self-doubt and let yourself make mistakes, knowing that by doing so, you're making progress toward your goals.

Of course, mistakes and failure don't feel good in the moment, and you should let yourself feel the disappointment that comes with them. But instead of letting your mistakes define your self-

97

worth and halting your progress, learn from them and let them motivate you even more to try again. Even if you fail over and over again, you're learning an important lesson each time that will diminish your fear and allow you to persist until you succeed.

CHAPTER SIX:
PUTTING OURSELVES FIRST

When this guide first mentioned self-love, we indicated that it's synonymous with self-care and that we need to learn how to take care of ourselves both physically and mentally so that we can love ourselves. Unfortunately, self-care hasn't always been a revered practice, especially for girls and women.

For hundreds of years, women and girls have been socialized to take care of everyone else before considering their own needs. This is ingrained in society even as we try to change the way people view a woman's role. The truth is, though, that there is no way for people to be able to adequately care for others if they don't take care of their needs first.

Self-care is not selfish, even if we grow up thinking it is. And it's more than just taking a spa day or doing something fun, although that's definitely a part of it. It's about checking in with your feelings toward yourself and ensuring you're doing the things that energize you so you can fully participate in your life.

WHERE WE DO IT

People (women and girls in particular) put themselves and their needs on the back burner in nearly every circumstance, but especially when it concerns their loved ones. They are trained to consider what they can do to help the people they love be happier, solve problems, and get through the tough times, and generally to support them in everything they do. We think that's what family does and certainly we should do what we can for them. But we shouldn't sacrifice our own well-being to make others' lives easier or better.

We often put others' needs before our own at school and work as well, mainly when we take on more than we have time for. Maybe we volunteer for every task or role because we worry that things won't get done otherwise. Or we let our teachers or bosses pile work onto us because we don't want them to think we're incapable of handling the load. Perhaps we have a fear of letting others down so we try to attend every sporting event, every drama production, and every club meeting we're invited to, even if we don't particularly enjoy those things.

In fact, accepting more responsibilities than we can reasonably manage can become a problem anywhere, and the more things we're involved in, like church, clubs, and organizations, the more prone we are to taking on more than is manageable. And if we think that doing everything is the key to getting a better job, making friends, or being respected, we're all the more susceptible to saying "yes" to everything.

WHY WE DO IT

We've already touched on some reasons why we don't put ourselves first, namely because we think it's selfish and because women in particular have been socialized to serve. But let's take a look at these reasons a little deeper and add a few more.

We Think Self-Care is Selfish

We associate self-care with selfishness because we have been conditioned to consider others first. In fact, many religions place a significant emphasis on caring for others as you would care for yourself. And even though this tenet of religion places care for others on the same level as self-care, the act of caring for others is frequently prioritized over caring for yourself.

In actuality, self-care is in no way selfish. You aren't harming anyone by taking time to fulfill your own needs. You aren't taking something away from another person to make yourself feel better. You simply can't properly care for others until you satisfy your own emotional, mental, physical, and spiritual needs. Once you reframe self-care as something that is necessary for you to be able to give to others, you can let go of the guilt you might feel for doing something that's good for you.

Women Are Socialized to Care for Others

Throughout Western civilization, women have been taught that others' needs should be taken care of first. One modern example is when women are expected to not only cook a meal for their family, but also to ensure everyone else eats before they do. Often, a woman ends up eating a cold meal because she's busy ensuring everyone else has eaten and is satisfied.

This perception of women is evident in many facets of life. Girls are encouraged to take classes that lead to careers in service industries, from hospitality or psychology, to nursing, education, or childcare. Women are supposed to be "good" at these things because they always put others first and when they don't, they're viewed as having something wrong with them.

For example, women who don't cook are thought to be poor marital options, especially by older generations that grew up expecting women to cook all the meals. These perceptions are changing, but they are still widespread enough to make women feel guilty about not adhering to gender norms or for taking time to care for themselves first.

We Want to Rescue Others

Who doesn't want to play the role of hero? We see someone in distress and we take it upon ourselves to save them, even if they don't want to be saved. This results in us taking on the responsibility for someone else's happiness at the expense of our own. We don't usually have time to ensure someone else is happy and that we're happy ourselves, so we may choose to sacrifice our own needs.

But rescuing someone from unpleasant experiences does nothing for either one of you. The other person doesn't have the chance to learn from their mistakes and you don't have the time or energy to take care of yourself. You aren't responsible for other people's happiness and if they want you to be, you might want to re-read the section on toxic people.

We Like Being Useful

Our desire to always be productive sometimes gets in our way of taking care of ourselves. We want to feel like others need us because it's a sign that we have value. But we need to remember that our self-worth is not dependent on sacrificing our needs for others. Sure, we should help other people whenever we can, but we should also help ourselves so that we have the energy and space to help others when the opportunity arises.

We need to have a purpose in life and, often, we associate taking care of others as our purpose. But that is short-sighted because we can only do so much for others before we're burned out and unable to give anymore. Our purpose should be to become the person we want by loving ourselves enough to take care of our needs. Once we've done that, we'll be in a better position to help those who really need it.

We Are Teaching Others How to Treat Us

When we show people that we're willing to sacrifice ourselves to make them happy or to fulfill their needs, we teach them that it's okay to take advantage of us. We will ultimately attract the type of people who want to be rescued and taken care of, which means the relationship you have with them (friendship or otherwise) will be all about them.

Eventually, you'll be unable to give these people everything they've become accustomed to receiving from you and they will likely get upset that you've changed the dynamics in the relationship. After all, are they really taking advantage of you if you're willingly giving to them? But by the time you get to this breaking point, you could be bitter and angry that you're doing all the giving and doing nothing for yourself.

Alternatively, when we take care of our own needs first, we show others that we value ourselves enough to do the things we need to recharge our batteries. We teach them that we have our boundaries that they need to respect and that, by doing so, we'll be a better friend because we won't be giving everything we have away. Most people will encourage your self-care because they realize you're a better person when you're taking the time to nourish your spirit.

We Want Others to Do the Same for Us

Giving to others should come from a place of love and not from any ulterior motives, but when we care for others to the point where we have nothing left to give ourselves, we are probably doing it because we expect others to give back to us to the same degree. Unfortunately, this almost never happens and when we don't get the same effort in return, we start to wonder if it's because we don't deserve it.

Interestingly, even if the other person does give back to you in equal amounts, you're still not going to be fulfilled because they can't give you the one thing you need: self-love. It's impossible for others to give you self-love because, as this guide has shown, self-love comes from within. Another person can give you everything they have, but there will still be a gap that only you can fill through the practice of self-care.

Self-care is your responsibility and you can't expect others to know what you need to take care of yourself. They might not even know that they're taking advantage of you when they don't return what you gave them in equal amounts. They just figure if you're going to give, then you want them to take.

Certainly, there will be some people who don't take advantage of your giving nature, but they still can't give you everything you need. There are some things that only you can give yourself.

We Don't Value Ourselves Enough

In the end, we put ourselves last because we may think other people are worth more than we are. We might not think we are worthy of investing in self-care so we don't do it until we're forced to because we've burned ourselves out. Even then, we usually don't give ourselves everything we need. We just do enough to get us back on our feet and caring for others again.

We've said it numerous times throughout this guide: you can't fully love others until you love yourself. Even if you think you are loving others by doing everything you can for them, you're not. When you accept and love yourself, though, you free yourself up to love others because you don't need someone else's love or approval. You'll know that the relationships you have are truly based on love and not your need for acceptance.

On the other hand, if you're unaccepting and critical of yourself, you might not believe that another person can love you or that you're worthy of love. You'll potentially hold part of yourself back just in case and you might even present yourself as something you're not as a way to earn their love. But then, they're not loving the real you anyway, so it's not authentic.

WHY WE
SHOULDN'T DO IT

We Get Burned Out

Putting ourselves last for care leads to burnout, resentment, and anger. You'll find yourself giving everything you have to others and not getting what you need in return. Eventually, you just won't be able to give any more and the shift in relationship dynamics may be even more harmful than if you hadn't given everything you had in the first place.

People will come to expect you to care for them before caring for yourself and may not understand when you change the rules. And if you don't change the rules, you'll become resentful and angry toward the people you're supposedly caring for. It's really a no-win situation when you don't take care of yourself first-- if not immediately, then definitely down the road.

We Have Less Patience

Burnout and low energy leads to frustration and a lack of patience, which can come out as anger or dismissiveness to other people. These emotions are the opposite of the person you're trying to be, but when you have no energy left to take care of yourself, you aren't the best version of yourself to anyone. Angry, bitter people are not popular and you'll enter the cycle of disliking yourself because people don't want to be around you.

It's Unhealthy — Both Physically and Mentally

As you already know, self-care is important for staying healthy and making healthy choices. Our brains are programmed to be more reactionary when our energy is low. This is the old "fight or flight" phenomenon, where our brains click into survival mode and make the decision that makes the most sense at the time. Unfortunately, that decision is often the unhealthy one.

For example, when we're burned out, it's much easier to choose to eat fast food than to be bothered to cook something healthy. We know what the healthy choice is, but in the moment our brain tells us to just get something to eat for survival. It doesn't matter what it is as long as it makes you feel better. Then, when we ultimately make the poor choice, we fall down the rabbit hole of criticizing ourselves for making a mistake or allowing the failure to affect our self-worth.

Along with making healthier choices, self-care allows us to sleep better because we're not focused on why we're not taking care of others and letting them down. Overall, taking care of ourselves before others puts us in a space where we are relaxed and happy, a healthy state of being.

When we aren't burned out from giving everything we have to others, we can actually be more productive as well. We have more energy to do the things we need to do for others because we've taken care of fulfilling ourselves and our needs. We aren't feeling like we're running in 10 different directions and can focus on each task as it comes. Stepping away from others' expectations of us allows us to recharge our batteries so we can meet more of those expectations.

We Miss Out on Experiences

Sacrificing what we need to do for ourselves and focusing on others also puts us in a position where we miss out on wonderful experiences that we need for self-care. For example, if traveling is something you do to relax and recharge, but you can't go anywhere because you're taking care of someone else, you're going to miss out on those opportunities. Missing out on things you want to be doing for yourself will feed into the angry and bitter feelings that come from neglecting your own needs.

We Become Reluctant to Try New Things

Additionally, you might be reluctant to try new things because you are either out of energy to give what is necessary for those new things or you pass them up because you don't want to interfere with your "job" of caring for others. You might feel trapped into the role you've set up for yourself and end up doing only the things others want to do.

Fortunately, you can start to get out from underneath the weight of caring for others before yourself. You just have to make some changes in your life and communicate your new approach to the people you've been catering to. These changes might be difficult, particularly for them, but they are necessary if you want to be the person you're meant to be, which will ultimately benefit everyone.

HOW TO
STOP DOING IT

Schedule Self-Care Time

The first change to make when you're shifting from caring for others first to caring for yourself is to actively schedule self-care time. You can't just say, "I'm going to start taking better care of myself" because that is too vague to work. It's always a good idea to set some goals around self-care so you can work toward what you ultimately want a step at a time.

Start by identifying the things that energize you, the things that give you joy, the things that never feel like work. Maybe it's reading or writing. Perhaps it's traveling or exercising. It could even be simply sitting on your porch doing nothing. Whatever you enjoy that allows you to stop the crazy ride you're on and get out of the heat for a while are the things you should put on your self-care list.

You'll also want to put some of the things we've discussed in this guide on your list as well, such as limiting social media time, showing yourself grace when you make a mistake, listening to your intuition, listing things you're grateful for, spending time with positive people, practicing mindfulness, and more. When you put all the tips for helping you love yourself together, you'll start to experience true self-love.

Do not allow yourself to cancel your self-care appointments, either. This will be tempting to do, at least at first, but it's critical for you to stick to your schedule. Doing so will show the people in your life that you're serious about taking time for yourself and that you really are going to prioritize self-care. They will be less likely to try to convince you to skip a self-care appointment once they realize how important it is to you.

Set Reasonable Goals

As with learning how to trust yourself, self-care requires you to set reasonable goals. They shouldn't be too easy to attain, but they also shouldn't be so far out of reach that you're basically killing yourself to reach them. When you set your goals too high, you'll burn yourself out trying to meet them and if you fail, you might enter the cycle of criticizing yourself for setting them too high or for not being good enough to accomplish them.

Be careful about the number of goals you set at any one time as well. You are busy and you're now adding time for self-care to your plate. This will decrease the amount of time you have to care for others, but also to make progress toward your goals. It's okay if you take longer to get where you're going because you'll be doing it in a healthier way. And remember, you'll ultimately be more productive when you take time for self-care because your energy levels will remain higher for a longer period of time.

Set Reasonable Boundaries

This is a big one for self-care. Setting reasonable boundaries with the people you've been giving yourself to is going to be vital for your self-care success. Keep in mind that they aren't going to want to change. They don't want to have to find someone else to do the things you used to do or figure out a way to do those things themselves. They may try to pressure you to "just do it one more time" or tell you that "this won't take long."

Those phrases are testing your boundaries to see if you're really serious about the change you're making. If you give in to them, even once, they'll know that you'll do it again when they need you to. Your boundaries need to be clearly communicated ("I'm not going to volunteer this semester because I need to focus on my own goals" or "I'm not going to fill in for people who can't make their work shifts on weekends because that's time for me to go camping with my family") and firmly enforced. When they are, people will start to respect them.

If people continue to violate your boundaries even after you've consistently enforced them, you may need to designate them as toxic and treat them as such. People who don't respect boundaries are not interested in helping you fulfill your self-love goals. They only see what you can do for them and when you're not doing that anymore, they have a hard time giving it up. They will continue to try to get things back the way they were, which means you'll need to limit your contact with them.

Learn to Say No

Learning to say no is setting a boundary, but it deserves its own section because it can be very hard to do. Again, we want people to like us and we want to please them, so we tend to say "yes" to everything we're asked to do. We also tend to want to avoid conflict and we fear that saying "no" will cause a problem. It's easier to say "yes," even if we know we don't want to do something or we don't have time to do it.

And, if you've been caring for others for a while, you might feel like saying "no" is letting them down, a feeling that can affect our self-worth. We might tell ourselves, "If I was worth anything, I wouldn't let people down." Of course, this isn't true because a major part of self-care is saying "no" to things you don't want to do in favor of saying "yes" to the things that nourish your soul.

We also live in a society where the people who say "yes" the most are viewed as "go-getters" and are considered more successful. But saying "yes" to things you really want to say "no" to will only breed resentment because you won't enjoy what you're doing, which quickly depletes your energy reserves. While saying "no" might be uncomfortable in the moment, it is actually the best thing for everyone involved because it preserves the relationship.

Participate in Activities You Enjoy

If you don't know where to start with self-care, begin by thinking about the things you enjoy doing. They might even be activities you did when you were a kid (coloring, building with LEGO, watching cartoons). Get back to the basics of what makes you happy so you can start understanding what recharges your batteries.

They don't have to be major activities such as going on an actual vacation or visiting a theme park, and you don't even have to spend money on them. Maybe you love being around water and just walking around a lake a few times or sitting next to a river is enough to give you the contented feeling you need.

Perhaps spending time with animals is what centers you and calms you down. If you don't have pets of your own, you can visit an animal shelter (for free) and get all the time with animals you need. Plus, they'll benefit from your interaction with them as well. Sometimes, you just need to think outside the box to find the activities you enjoy.

Ask the people in your lives about opportunities to participate in activities you think you'll love. For example, if you're really into creating art, talk to the art teacher at your school about clubs or events that allow attendees to paint, draw, or sculpt. If reading certain kinds of books puts you in a relaxed and contented mood, ask a librarian for recommendations.

Remember that the people in your life generally want the best for you and will help you find activities that feed your sense of self-love. You don't have to do it all on your own and in fact, you may not know exactly which activities you enjoy until you have the opportunity to try some out.

Take Opportunities

When you have the opportunity to try something new, take it. You might be scared or nervous about what's going to happen or of failing, but you also might just discover your next passion. The famous hockey player Wayne Gretsky once said, "you miss 100% of the shots you don't take." In other words, you'll never know what you're missing out on if you don't try new things.

Middle school and high school are the perfect times to participate in things you've never tried before. There are hundreds of opportunities in your school and community for clubs, events, and other activities that allow you to expand your horizons. Many of these things are free or low cost because they want people to participate.

When you get older, you're going to have less time to try new things because you'll be busy with your career and/or raising a family. You won't have as much access to free opportunities either. Even if you aren't sure if you'd like an activity that your school offers, give it a chance. You might not enjoy it and you'll know for sure, or it will surprise you and you'll add it to your self-care list.

Spend Time with Your Family and Friends

One of the best things we can do to take care of ourselves is to spend time with the people we love and who love us back for who we are. Most of the time, this circle includes our family members and close friends, but it really doesn't matter who is included as long as they are good for you.

The people you should spend time with as part of your self-care routine are those that don't expect anything from you except friendship and love. They aren't going to demand you give to them without them giving back to you in equal amounts. You'll laugh a lot with this group and you'll feel better and more energized when you leave them than you did before you hung out with them.

You may not have a lot of these people in your life, and that's perfectly okay. You only need a few people who love you for who you really are to gain the benefits of their friendship. Keep in mind that you probably do the same things for them that they do for you. In other words, you make them feel good about their true selves.

We can't always spend as much time with these people in person as we'd like, but with today's technology, we can still get the benefits of their friendship. Text with them and talk to them on the phone. Set up video calls and participate in the same activity together while you're on the call with them. For instance, watch your favorite television show together and discuss it in real time. Play online games together or participate in a group chat about the most recent book you've all read.

While the advent of the Internet hasn't all been good, it can definitely be a boon for self-care, particularly if your friends don't live in the same town. Take advantage of this technology to make sure you're able to get what you need from their friendship. Fortunately, your brain can't tell the difference between online interaction and in-person interaction when it comes to self-love.

Spend Time by Yourself

Not only should you spend time with others who make you feel good about yourself, but you should spend time by yourself as well. Many people struggle with being alone, but it's an important part of self-care. Why? It's about silencing the world around you and listening to your inner self. It's about becoming comfortable with being a friend to yourself, something you can't do when your brain is occupied with the busyness and loudness of the world.

When you're spending time by yourself, you don't have to do anything. You can just sit and think, or meditate if you want. You can spend this time in your room or in another space that provides a buffer between you and other people. Maybe you like sitting on a bench in the park or on the steps to your back porch. Choose a place where you're unlikely to be interrupted by other people or technology for a set amount of time. Again, schedule this time by yourself so you don't fill it in with other obligations.

However, if you don't want to just sit and think, you can do other things by yourself. Write in a journal. Listen to music. Cook. Dance. Ride your bike. As long as you're doing it alone, you're allowing yourself to pause the world and recharge your energy.

Your alone time can also be ideal for setting goals. When you're able to listen to your inner voice, you can really focus on what it is you want to achieve. It's the perfect time to let your imagination run wild as you consider your dreams. What is the next step toward making them a reality? What do I need to reach that next goal? How much time should I give myself to reach it? These are all great questions that you can think about without interruption when you're by yourself.

Say the affirmations you need to build yourself up from the inside. Speak kindly and encourage yourself to keep progressing toward the person you want to be. No one is going to think you're strange for doing this when you're doing it alone, and your body and brain will be still enough to listen carefully to and internalize what you're telling yourself. Alone time is ideal to practice self-love while practicing self-care at the same time.

CONCLUSION

Loving yourself is a lifelong journey. We all have times when we're not sure if we like ourselves or not, but the key is to acknowledge these feelings and explore where they are coming from. Are we comparing ourselves to others? Are we worrying about what others are thinking of us? Are we putting our self-worth in our body? Are we holding onto toxic people? Are we doubting ourselves? Are we putting ourselves last?

Whatever we're doing to not like ourselves at any given moment, we need to take corrective action to stop that feeling in its tracks. We can't let it fester and grow because the longer we let sabotaging behaviors go unchecked, the harder it will be to get back to a point where we love ourselves.

The problem is that we tell ourselves literally thousands of messages every single day and if we don't notice that those messages are negative, we're chipping away at our self-love without even realizing it. This is why it's critical to check in throughout the day to make sure you're feeling good about yourself.

Mindfulness is a tip this guide has given as the antidote for sabotaging behaviors and we're going to mention it again here because of the power it has to change your thinking. Your goal is to make sure that most of those thousands of messages you're sending to your brain every day are positive, but this takes a lot of practice. Mindfulness is that practice.

At first, you might have to schedule times to check in throughout the day. Before school or work and after school or work are excellent times because so much happens during the day that your feelings about yourself can change throughout those hours.

Before school or work, ask yourself how you're feeling about anything that's coming up. Are you nervous? Excited? Uncertain? Why are you having those feelings? Are you doubting yourself? Comparing yourself to others? When you identify the answers to those questions, you can use the tips in this guide to counteract the sabotaging behaviors.

After school or work, ask yourself how you're feeling after everything that's happened during the day. Be honest with yourself and again, when you have the answers, use this guide to help you overcome any sabotaging behaviors you're engaging in. Eventually, you'll be able to quickly check in with yourself at any time during the day without scheduling special mindfulness times.

You also might need help understanding what sabotaging behaviors you're engaging in, especially if you are young and haven't had many life experiences yet. Remember that you are not on this self-love journey alone. The people in your life want you to love yourself because you deserve it. You are worthy of self-love.

Talk to your family and close friends about your quest to love yourself and ask them to help you along the way. They can and will help you come up with affirmations. They will help you set goals and boundaries. They will help you identify the reasons behind your feelings. The more people who are by your side while you work toward self-love, the better your life will ultimately be.

Made in United States
North Haven, CT
21 December 2022

29898540R00075